Meet my neighbor, the builder

Marc Crabtree

Author and Photographer

🎋 Crabtree Publishing Company

www.crabtreebooks.com

Crabtree Publishing Company

Meet my neighbor, the builder

For Stephen and Karen, with thanks

Author and Photographer
Marc Crabtree

Editor
Reagan Miller

Design
Samantha Crabtree

Production coordinator
Margaret Amy Salter

Glossary
Crystal Sikkens

Photographs
All photographs by Marc Crabtree

Library and Archives Canada Cataloguing in Publication

Crabtree, Marc
    Meet my neighbor, the builder / author and photographer, Marc Crabtree.

(Meet my neighbor)
ISBN 978-0-7787-4580-8 (pbk.).--ISBN 978-0-7787-4570-9 (bound)

    1. Stewart, Stephen--Juvenile literature. 2. House construction--Juvenile literature. 3. Construction workers--Biography--Juvenile literature. I. Title. II. Series: Crabtree, Marc . Meet my neighbor.

TH4811.5.C73 2009   j690.092   C2009-900421-6

Library of Congress Cataloging-in-Publication Data

Crabtree, Marc.
  Meet my neighbor, the builder / author and photographer, Marc Crabtree.
       p. cm. -- (Meet my neighbor)
   ISBN 978-0-7787-4580-8 (pbk. : alk. paper) -- ISBN 978-0-7787-4570-9 (reinforced library binding : alk. paper)
   1. House construction--Juvenile literature. I. Title.
   TH4811.5.C73 2009
   690'.8--dc22

                                  2009001568

Crabtree Publishing Company

www.crabtreebooks.com   1-800-387-7650

Published in Canada
Crabtree Publishing
616 Welland Ave.
St. Catharines, Ontario
L2M 5V6

Published in the United States
Crabtree Publishing
PMB16A
350 Fifth Ave., Suite 3308
New York, NY 10118

Published in the United Kingdom
Crabtree Publishing
White Cross Mills
High Town, Lancaster
LA1 4XS

Published in Australia
Crabtree Publishing
386 Mt. Alexander Rd.
Ascot Vale (Melbourne)
VIC 3032

Contents

Meet my Neighbor

Meet my neighbor, Stephen Stewart, the builder. Stephen is sitting at home with his wife Karen, his son, Jordan, and his daughter, Lauren. Their dog's name is Hailey.

After a long day of working
as builders and going to school,
Stephen and his family are hungry.

Both Stephen and Karen own a building company.

This house was damaged in a fire. Stephen and Karen are fixing it.

This team of workers will help Stephen and Karen fix the house.

Stephen buys **wood** at the lumber store.

Stephen loads the wood into his truck. His **ladders** are on top of the truck.

Stephen builds the **frame** of the house with wood. The frame holds up the walls and roof.

These workers use a **safety harness**. They will not fall off the roof.

15

These workers hold up a wall while another worker nails it into place.

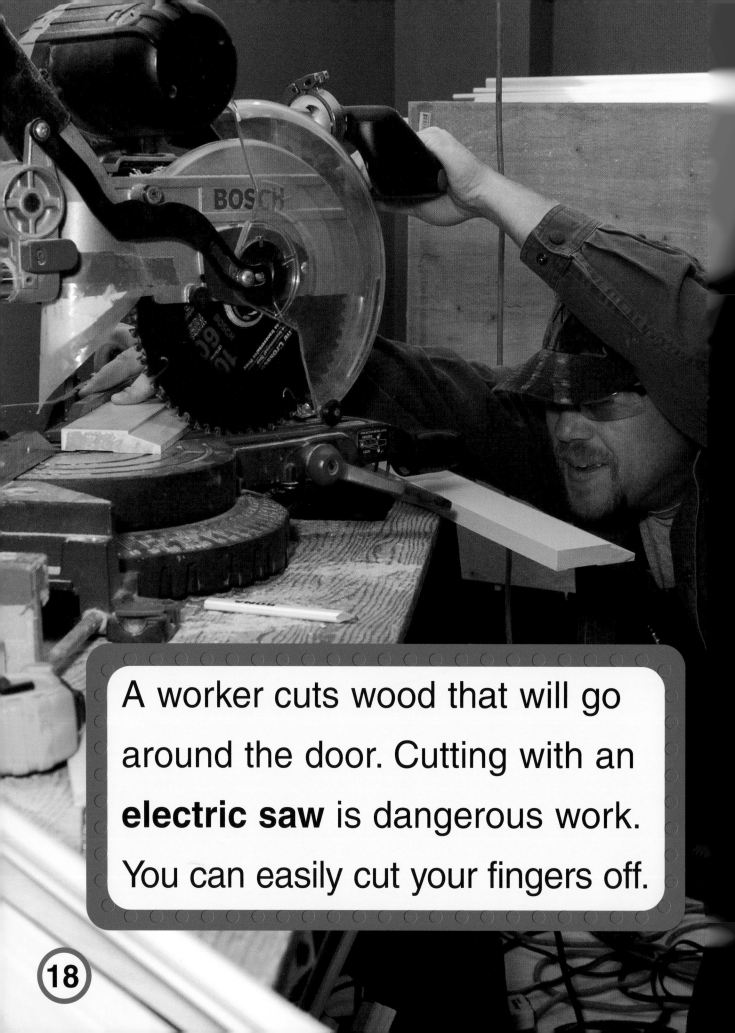

A worker cuts wood that will go around the door. Cutting with an **electric saw** is dangerous work. You can easily cut your fingers off.

Stephen puts the wood around a new door.

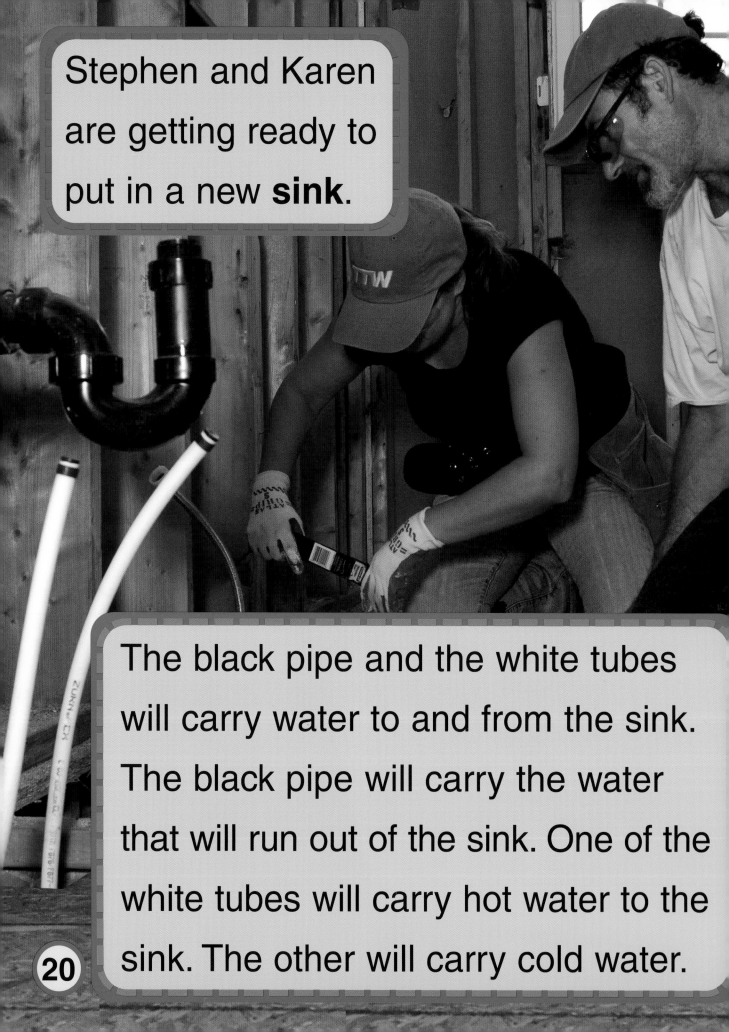

Stephen and Karen are getting ready to put in a new **sink**.

The black pipe and the white tubes will carry water to and from the sink. The black pipe will carry the water that will run out of the sink. One of the white tubes will carry hot water to the sink. The other will carry cold water.

20

Karen carries wood destroyed in the fire to Stephen's truck.

A worker uses a **bulldozer** to fix the lawn and gardens.

Glossary

bulldozer

electric saw

frame

ladder

harness

safety harness

sink

wood

Printed in the U.S.A. - CG